MOUNTAIN MAMMALS

A TRUE BOOK

by

Elaine Landau

D0756741

Children's Press®
A Division of Grolier Publishing

New York London Hong Kong Sydney
Danbury, Connecticut

For Bianca, Jerry, and Abraham

Reading Consultant
Linda Cornwell
Learning Resource Consultant
Indiana Department of
Education

Subject Consultant
Kathy Carlstead, Ph.D.
National Zoological Park
Smithsonian Institution

Pikas live among the
cracks in mountain rocks.

Library of Congress Cataloging-in-Publication Data

Landau, Elaine.
   Mountain mammals / by Elaine Landau.
      p.   cm. — (A true book)
   Includes bibliographical references and index.
   Summary: Briefly describes such animals as pikas, yaks, giant pandas,
and vicunas that live in various mountain ranges around the world.
   ISBN 0-516-20040-2 (lib. bdg.)   ISBN 0-516-26109-6 (pbk.)
   1. Mountain animals—Juvenile literature. 2. Mammals—Juvenile litera-
ture. [1. Mountain animals.] I. Title. II. Series.
QL113.L35 1996
599—dc20   96-3893
                                                              CIP
                                                              AC

Contents

The Rocky Mountains of
the United States

Mountain Mammals

The mountains of the world are home to many mammals. Mammals are animals with backbones and with larger brains than other types of animals. Mammals are also the only animals that nurse their young. The greatest number of mountain mammals

It is too cold for trees to grow above the timberline.

is usually found near the foot of the mountain. Bears, deer, and elk thrive in these rich forest areas and grassy valleys.

Fewer animals live at the higher mountain locations, where it is rainy and colder. Above the point known as the timberline, even trees cannot grow. Only some shrubs, mosses, and plants can survive on these rocky cliffs, so there is less food for wildlife. A few animals, such as some insects and spiders, live on the mountains' icy peaks, and sometimes an eagle soars by.

This book introduces some interesting mountain mammals in their habitats. Sadly, in some cases their future on the mountain may not be as sure as their past.

Few animals live on a mountain's icy peaks.

Bighorn sheep are found in western Canada and the United States.

Canada

NORTH AMERICA

United States

CENTRAL AMERICA

EU

A F R

SOUTH AMERICA

Peru

Vicunas are found in the Andes Mountains of Peru, Bolivia, Chile, and Argentina.

Bolivia

Argentina

Chile

N

W   E

S

ANTAR

Giant pandas live in the bamboo forests of the mountains of central China.

ASIA

China

Tibet

Pikas are found in central Asia and western North America.

Yaks are found in Tibet and nearby areas of eastern central Asia.

AUSTRALIA

ROPE

ICA

CTICA

Pikas

The pika is a furry, grayish brown mammal with a white or beige underside. It grows from 5 to 7 inches (13 to 18 centimeters) long and usually weighs under 1 pound (453 grams). With its large head, round body, and short legs, the pika looks a lot like a guinea pig.

12

A pika peeks out of its burrow.

Pikas are always alert for danger.

Pikas live above the timber-line in groups called colonies. These animals warn one another with a loud squeaky cry if an enemy, such as an eagle or weasel, approaches. Then, the pikas flee for cover.

14

Usually they hide beneath an overhanging rock or within a crack in the rocks.

Pikas eat nearly any type of available plant growth. They survive the freezing mountain winters by storing enough

A pika carries food back to its burrow for the winter.

A pika munches on elderberries.

food for the season. In the fall, they gather berries, twigs, leaves, thistles, and pine needles. They leave these piles of food out to dry in the sun. Before winter sets in, the pikas bring the food to their rocky burrows. There, they remain snug, warm, dry, and well fed during the colder months.

Pika young are usually born between May and September. They must learn quickly to take care of themselves. Those born too late to gather enough food may not make it through the winter.

A pika waits out the snowy winter.

Bighorn Sheep

The bighorn is a wild North American mountain sheep. Its size and color vary depending on where it lives. The large bighorns in the north are gray-ish brown. Male bighorns, or rams, measure 3 to 4 feet (1 to 1.2 meters) high at the shoulder and weigh up to 350 pounds (160 kilograms). Light beige

Bighorn sheep have large, curled horns.

A herd of bighorns graze in a meadow.

bighorns in the desert mountains to the south are smaller.
Both types have creamy white
undersides and rumps.

Bighorns walk across the
mountains' rolling foothills and
graze in their meadows. But
these sure-footed animals do
not stray far from the mountains' rocky slopes. This allows
these excellent cliff jumpers to
flee quickly if necessary.
Bighorns have been known to
leap as far as 17 feet (5 m) to
escape from an enemy.

Bighorn rams mainly use their horns to fight one another. These fights take place during the mating season, and the ram with the largest horns usually wins. For the next month, he mates with the females, called ewes, and acts as head of the herd.

After mating, the males and females separate according to age. Female bighorns and their newborns remain in their own herds. Adult males go off alone.

Rams fight each other at mating time.

Bighorn sheep and their young

Bighorn sheep follow certain routes to reach their grazing pastures. The older sheep show the young bighorns the proper paths and feeding zones. In recent

times, however, humans inter-
rupted this process when they
began to farm many of the areas
once used by wild bighorns.

With farmers grazing their livestock on the same meadows,
the available food supply shrank.
Many bighorns suffered from
poor nutrition and diseases.
Before long, the bighorn popu-
lation decreased. Programs to
restore their habitat have been
started and are vital to the
bighorn's survival.

Yaks

The yak is a large, shaggy mountain ox. An adult male measures about 6 feet (1.8 m) high at the shoulder and weighs about 1,200 pounds (545 kg). The wild yak has a long, thick coat of brownish black hair. Its long horns curve upward and measure 30 to 40 inches (76 to 102 cm) across.

26

A shaggy yak in Tibet

Yaks prefer cold climates. They stay on the cold snowy mountains in the summers (above), and only move down to the valleys during winters (right).

During warm months, yaks remain on the snow-covered mountain slopes of eastern central Asia at heights of about 20,000 feet (6,100 m). In the freezing winters, they move lower down on the mountains to graze in the valleys. There, they feed on grass and small shrubs.

The number of wild yaks has sharply decreased over the years. But many domestic yaks live in the Asian country of Tibet. Domestic yaks are smaller

A yak in the Altai Mountains of Mongolia

than wild yaks, and they are usually either red or brown and white. Tibetan people often ride on these yaks to travel from place to place and also use them to carry goods. Domestic yaks are also used for their rich milk and meat. Yak hides are used for cloth and leather products as well.

Yaks are used to carry goods in Asia.

Giant Pandas

The giant panda, a large black-and-white mammal, has appealed to people throughout the world for generations. The panda was even a model for a popular teddy bear, known as the panda bear.

In the wild, giant pandas live only in China's cool, damp, bamboo forests. These

Pandas are known for their unique markings (left). They live in the bamboo forests of China (above).

animals grow from 5 to 6 feet (1.5 to 1.8 m) tall and weigh up to 300 pounds (136 kg). While they seem somewhat

Pandas climb high into trees to feed (above). Bamboo shoots are their main source of food (left).

clumsy on the ground, pandas are outstanding climbers. They often climb bamboo trees to pick their main source of food—bamboo shoots.

Each year, adult pandas eat up to fifty times their weight in bamboo. They spend most of their time eating and only stop for about ten hours a day to sleep. They take several short naps during the day or night.

Pandas usually live by them-selves in an area about 1.5 to 2.5 square miles (4 to 6.5 square

A panda sits back to rest.

kilometers) in size. But male and female pandas do spend a short time together each year during the mating season. Females give birth to one or two cubs. Usually, when two panda cubs are born, only one of them survives. These fragile, hairless newborns are extremely small and weigh only 2.5 to 5 ounces (71 to 142 g).

Today, there are only about one thousand pandas in the wild. Many of their bamboo forests have been cut down to make room for farms. And, even though

Pandas are protected at the
Wolong Nature Reserve in China.

laws protect pandas, these animals are still illegally hunted.

The Chinese people have tried to save the pandas. Today, a number of panda reserves protect the panda's natural setting. Laws protecting the animal are also strictly enforced. China regards the panda as one of its national treasures.

37

Vicunas

The vicuna is the smallest member of the camel family. This long-necked, slender mountain mammal measures 2 to 3 feet (0.6 to 0.9 m) high at the shoulder and weighs 80 to 135 pounds (36 to 61 kg).

This grass-eating animal lives in the Andes Mountains

Vicunas are members of
the camel family.

Vicunas graze in Peru (above). A herd of vicunas runs across a rocky slope (right).

of South America. It is generally found in small herds at mountain heights ranging from 12,000 to 16,000 feet (3,700 to 4,900 m).

Throughout history, humans have been intrigued by the vicuna. At one time, it was worshiped as a holy animal. Later, the Inca Indians of Peru used the vicuna's wool to make special garments for their leaders. In time, the vicuna came to be viewed as a

money-making product. By the early 1800s, large numbers of vicunas were being killed for their fleece and their skins.

Laws were passed in 1825 to stop the killing, but these regulations were often ignored. In recent years, stronger legal measures have been taken. In Bolivia and Peru, national parks have been established where the vicuna can live safely. Hopefully, such actions will save this animal from extinction.

Humans have always been fascinated by the slender vicuna.

To Find Out More

Here are more places to learn about mountain mammals.

 **Books**

Arnold, Caroline. **Panda.** Morrow Junior Books, 1992.

Few, Roger. **Macmillan's Children's Guide to Endangered Animals.** Macmillan, 1993.

George, Jean Craighead. **One Day in the Alpine Tundra.** Crowell, 1984.

Lasky, Kathryn. **Think Like an Eagle: At Work with a Wildlife Photographer.** Little, Brown, 1992.

Maynard, Thane. **Saving Endangered Mammals: A Field Guide to Some of the Earth's Rarest Animals.** Franklin Watts, 1992.

Patent, Dorothy Hinshaw. **Places of Refugee: Our National Wildlife Refuge System.** Clarion Books, 1992.

Reynolds, Jan. **Himalaya: Vanishing Cultures.** Harcourt, Brace & Jovanovich, 1991.

Simon, Seymour. **Mountains.** Morrow Junior Books, 1994.

 **Organizations**

National Park Service
Office of Public Inquiries
P.O. Box 37127
Washington, DC 20013
(202) 208-4747

North Cascades National Park

2105 State Route 20
Sedro-Woolley, WA 98284
(360) 856-5700
http://www.halcyon.com/rd
payne/ncnp-mammals.html

Sierra Club

730 Polk Street
San Francisco, CA 94109
(415) 776-2211
http://www.sierraclub.org/

Smithsonian: National Zoological Park

3000 block of Connecticut
  Avenue, NW
Washington, DC 20008
(202) 673-4800
http://www.si.sgi.com/
perspect.afafam/afazoo.htm

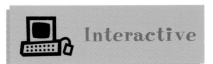

Interactive

Mammals: A Multimedia Encyclopedia.

National Geographic Society. Discover photos, videos, and sounds of hundreds of mammals—from aardvarks to zebras!
Ages 7+

The San Diego Zoo Presents: The Animals!

The Software Toolworks. Explore every part of this zoo as you see and learn about your favorite animals.
Ages 8+

Electronic Zoo

http://www.zi.biologie.
uni-muenchen.de/~st2042/
exotic.html
Visit the zoo without leaving home!

Great Panda Bears

http://www.ladue.k12.mo.us
/Wildwatch/bear/panda.html
Learn all about these beautiful, exotic bears.

Fish & Wildlife Service

http://www.fws.gov//
bio-walr.html
Enter a world of information on all kinds of animals.

Rocky Mountain Bighorn Society

http://spot.colorado.
edu/~kozar/Sheep.html
Unearth pictures, information, and publications about bighorn sheep.

Important Words

burrow hole in the ground made by an animal for shelter

domestic tame

extinction no longer existing

foothill low hill at the base of a mountain

fragile delicate

habitat an animal's environment

herd a group of animals

livestock farm animals

shrub thick, low-growing bush

timberline point on a mountain above which trees will not grow

wildlife untamed animals living in their natural environment

Index

Meet the Author

Elaine Landau worked as a newspaper reporter, children's book editor, and youth services librarian before becoming a full-time writer. She has written more than ninety books for young people.

Ms. Landau lives within New Jersey's Kittatinny Mountain range. She enjoys the mountain views from her home, as well as daily backyard visits from a number of different animals.

Photo Credits ©: Ben Klaffke: cover, 1, 10 top, 19; Dr. E. R. Degginger: 39, 42; George Stewart: 10–11 (map); Photo Researchers: 28 top (Art Twomey), 31 (Bill Liske), 28 bottom, 34 inset (both photos Fletcher & Baylis), 4, 24, 40 top (all photos Francois Gohier), 30 (George Holton), 11 bottom, 27 (both photos Kenneth W. Fink), 9 (Ted Kerasote), 6 (Teri Stratford), 11 top center, 33 inset, 34, 35, 37 (all photos Tim Davis), 15, 20, 23, 33 top (all photos Tom & Pat Lesson), 40 bottom (Ziesler/Jacana); Tom Stack & Associates: 10 bottom (Gary Milburn), 43 (Warren Garst/Wildlife Enterprises); Visuals Unlimited: 2 (Will Troyer), 14, 17 (both photos Barbara Gerlach), 13 (R. Lindholm), 11 top right, 16 (both photos William J. Weber).